Joanne S. Duffin has been a writer nearly all her life, from her early days at Riverside Polytechnic High School in California, under the excellent tutelage of Mr. William Bell in Honours English, to the present. However, it wasn't until ten years ago that she accepted a challenge from her husband to try her hand at poetry. Since then, she has written poetry for herself and others. She has been married for 43 years and is the proud mother of four grown children and eight grandchildren. A Renaissance woman, Joanne is also an award-winning photographer, a published author, a songwriter, an entrepreneur, an enthusiastic gardener, and loves interior design.

Marcus L. Duffin began writing poetry in 2007, shortly after venturing off on his own to find his path, personally and professionally, while starting graduate school. It was during this period of transition and growth that he felt inspired to put his thoughts and emotions onto paper to describe the changes happening in his life. As of today, he has been with his wife for 9 years and they have an 18-month-old son. He is an owner of three companies and has one pending and two issued patents. For fun, he enjoys inventing, anything outdoors, and going on motorcycle tours.

Joanne would like to dedicate this book to the ultimate poet, her father, Vinson Douglas Stephenson, who gifted her with his poetry throughout her life.

Marcus would like to dedicate this book to two people who provided him with guidance and inspiration during his life and the construction of his poetry. Mahatma Gandhi taught that anyone can become the change they wish to see in this world and this perspective truly helped him overcome times of adversity. He would also like to thank the original author of the *Serenity Prayer*, who taught him to be patient and accept the changes happening in his life.

Joanne S. Duffin and Marcus L. Duffin

SPILLING THE INK OF MY SOUL

A MOTHER AND SON'S JOURNEY

AUSTIN MACAULEY PUBLISHERS™

LONDON • CAMBRIDGE • NEW YORK • SHARJAH

Ordering Information
Quantity sales: Special discounts are available on quantity purchases by corporations, associations, and others. For details, contact the publisher at the address below.

Publisher's Cataloging-in-Publication data
Duffin, Joanne S. and Duffin, Marcus L.
Spilling the Ink of My Soul

ISBN 9781643786445 (Paperback)
ISBN 9781643782089 (Hardback)
ISBN 9781641829618 (ePub e-book)

Library of Congress Control Number: 2020912225

www.austinmacauley.com/us

First Published (2020)
Austin Macauley Publishers LLC
40 Wall Street, 28th Floor
New York, NY 10005
USA

mail-usa@austinmacauley.com
+1 (646) 5125767

Special thanks to:

Mr. William Bell
(Honours English teacher, Riverside Polytechnic
High School, Riverside, California, 1972–1973)

Carol Lynn Pearson
(Author, poet, and playwright)

Dr. Steven R. Duffin
(Husband)

Alfred Lord Tennyson
(Poet, specifically his poem "Ulysses")

Family

Your Beginning
For Maddox

You began as a thought
A wish, a prayer.
Warm and round
Pure and everlasting, you came
From the shallows of our hopes
To the depths of our longings.

How could we have known
Your entrance into the light
Would herald a new day
A new life
A vision of eternity
For three separate souls
Now made one:
A unit, a family.

We hold you tenderly
Feel your warmth
Skin to skin
Upon our breasts
The dream remaining

Paramount and sacred
In our grateful hearts.

Oh, that we, as your parents
Your guardians
Will bless and guide you!
Oh, that your eyes will open
Potential realized
Love, known!

Feel, oh son
The dawn of your awakening!
Look to the future:
Your vision clear of impediment
Your past, a distant echo
Of your former life.

From God
You have been sent
Wrapped in forgetfulness
The Book of Life opened
Ready for experience
The elixir of life
To be revealed to you!
Yes, this is your beginning!

Child of Light

As morning breaks
You are born
Out of the womb's darkness
Into life's light.

From the mountain tops
Has come the news of your birth
Heralding to all
Your joyous entrance into the world.

For such a day as this
You have come forth
Your purpose clear
Your talents known.

You are swaddled in blankets
By the clear light of love
As familiar voices
Whisper their ancient songs.

Hear now your mother's longing
That echoes in your slumber.
Hear now the low timbre
Of your father's wishes
And the tender cadence
Of your brother's prayer.

You are now blessed
With a family's kiss
Upon your cheeks of gold
And nurtured
On your mother's breast
With the milk of wisdom and knowledge.

Listen well, young son
To those who will serve you
In this world.
Listen well to the words
That will guide you home.

Now, fret not
Your temporary blindness
All will be revealed.
Forgetfulness will give way
And clarity of vision
Will be yours
As if a diamond of truth.

So, welcome child of light!
Welcome to your earthly home!

Fingerprints

The mirror
Faithfully reflects my image
Day after day
Since you've been gone.
To a stranger
One might think
I live alone
For there is little evidence
Beyond your clothes
Neatly hanging in the closet
That another lives here.

Last week
I cleaned the mirror
Where once your fingerprints lingered
But they have been wiped away
As though you never existed at all.
Now, as days turn into weeks
And you are still gone
I am missing those fingerprints

The tiny, oily stains
That are distinctly yours
Bearing a code unique to you!

Your mother once told me
She kept fingerprints of our children
Long after our visits…
Kept them up
Those smeared, swirled reminders
Of love and familial experience
To keep the memories alive longer…

I am yearning for you
Looking now purposefully
For other oily stains of you
Fingerprints of love
To bring you home to my heart.
These fingerprints
Will remain untouched
Physical reminders of you
No cloth will wipe away!

I will be here when you return!
It is then our arms
Will lock in sweet embrace
And our fingerprints
With their ancient dialect
Will be intertwined, once again!

Fireflies

For Al and Colleen

Bedtime comes
Soft and gentle.
The noise of today
Coalesces into a whisper
As summer's night
Eases into a cool decrescendo.

Outside a young father
The oldest in a family
Of thirteen children
Smells the thick Southern air
Bedecked with climbing roses
Wisteria, and peonies
And waits until the light of day dims
For his prize to appear.

In her crib lies his daughter, two
Afraid of the dark.
He cannot always be with her
When the sun's rays fade
And darkness falls.

As a young boy
And the eldest
He discovered
To the delight of his younger siblings
A way to capture light
And keep it
Sustain it through the night
Like magic fairy dust
Sprinkled about…

On this night
The sunset is brilliant
And the last vestiges of color are
Nearly gone.
In the air, they appear before him
The tiny fireflies
Their bodies pulsating with light.
One by one he gathers them
Cupped in his hand
And tenderly places them
In a simple Ball jar.

As night's blackness
Caresses the valleys and hillsides
Of Mother Earth
The jar of fireflies
Lights his path home.

There his daughter stirs in her crib
Whimpering still as darkness
Envelops her.

Around the door frame he appears
Bearing light.
Magically, she lies still
And watches as light dances
Within the jar!

Her father brings it closer
And tells her of the brave little warriors, the fireflies
That will protect her
Through the night…
But, how
At first light
They must be freed
To return home to their families.
Eyes half-mast, she settles
And is soon fast asleep.

The legend of the fireflies
Told to unbelieving Westerners
Unfolds before my eyes.
Its glow that flickers
In the blackness
Of a Southern night is true!
For I, a witness
Know now it is so!

Africa

Ghana! Dear Ghana!

You are in my thoughts
Ghana! Dear Ghana!
As I wake to the sunrise
Heralding the new day
I ruminate
On the unparalleled adventures
That await

Of Lake Volta
And hippopotami
Of monkeys dangling from vines
And warm cinnamon faces smiling
Against a jungle of green

Of warm rain showers
And Kente weaving
Of colorful beads
That adorn necks and wrists

Of Kings and Chieftains
Rich with Ewe language
And culture, and tradition.

I will think of this faraway land
This earth within an earth
And dream of my new home
Where I will live and love
Against a backdrop of
Red earth and teeming jungle.

I come to you now
With my eyes anxious for your colors
My palette ready for the exotic
And my heart wide open!
Hear my footsteps as I approach!
See me walk upon your soil of red!
I am here now in your rich land
With your warm people.
Envelope me now!
I kneel before you!
Ghana! Dear Ghana!

The Children's Smiles

They greet us every morning
Sleepy, we turn in our beds
Wipe our eyes
Focus on their faces
And see their smiles.

They know they are loved
Cherished
Wanted!
They give us a matchless gift
One that touches us
Like no other
Their smiles.

Who taught them to love?
Who taught them
That it is enough
To love with their eyes
Their mouths
Their hearts wide open?

It is no small wonder
That their gift is universally so
The children's smiles
Yet it is so!
It is no wonder
That material wealth
Is never what they are smiling about!
It is love!

The children's smiles
Are not rare
But they are priceless
Precious diamonds
Gifts beyond compare!

I've Passed Through Your Door
For Veronica

How many times
Have I passed through your door?
Followed the dirt road
And traversed the village paths
That lead to your doorstep?

How often have I found you there
Arms outstretched in welcome
Savory aromas wafting out from
The screened windows and open doorway?

You've greeted me in years past
With Jennifer, your charge.
But she is gone now
Gone home to find her way in the world.
Now Gifty greets us and invites us in.

I've passed through your door
As have so many others
Intersecting lives breaking bread together
Sharing stories, local folklore, and traditions.

People of all backgrounds
Have passed through your door, too
And painted their secrets
On your wall of time
Sharing histories rich
With adventure and dreams.

I speak my truth
Cloistered within the walls
Beyond your door
For love is spoken here.

Yes, I have passed through your door
And, if you, my friend, are willing
I will pass through them again
For our kinship is unequivocal
And our love and friendship
Divine.

I Will Sing a Song of Ghana

As the fading light of this day
Draws to a close
My time in Ghana
Is beginning to fade, too
As my memories separate
The recent past from the present.
I know my efforts at reverie
Will keep thoughts of you alive
For my heart and mind wish it so.

I will sing a song of Ghana
And remember
Your verdant jungles
Your children, whose smiles
Stretch beyond infinity
The beauty of your rivers and fields
As sunset falls at eventide
The thunderous monsoon rains
That swell your rivers
And overflow their banks.

I will sing a song of Ghana
For its voice echoes in my heart
And reverberates within the walls of my womb!
Awake and arise again, oh Ghana!
The whole world waits
For your diurnal rebirth
As morning breaks
On tender blades of green
And soil of red!

Mandela

Have I ever truly known what it is
To be fearless and brave?
To choose a path of resistance and consequence
For the sake of an ideal?
To forgive, without hatred or bitterness
An unrelenting oppressor?
Mandela did!

Have I ever been imprisoned, unjustly?
Tormented by captors?
Stripped of all earthly possessions?
Denied the comfort of family and friends for decades?
Mandela was!

A Moses for his people!
Born in a time of discontent
Strife, war, racism, apartheid!
A David, he stared down the mighty Goliath.
Unafraid, with only his rock of truth
And a slingshot of justice and indignation
Mandela felled the giant
And freed ALL people.

The flame of conviction
has burned within me
At various times in my life:
I have stood and faced many giants
And often times felt fear
Bearing down upon me.
I too have sought strength
Like David of old.

In the stillness of such moments
His face has appeared before me
Dark as the soil of Africa
And beckoned me to rise
And choose my rock
And, taking careful aim
Release it
And vanquish my foe!

Philosophical

The Creative Fire

Nighttime falls
And all is quiet and calm
As I sit by the fire
To warm myself
On such a chilly night as this.

I ponder the starlit sky
Through paned window
And marvel at the mystery
Of the infinite universe
That stretches before me.

Is not my own mind
As vast as the starlit night?
As complex and magical
And, yes, infinite and expansive
As the universe beyond?

Is not my fertile mind
As much a gift
As the fire that warms me?
As fathomless with creative possibilities

As the deepest ocean?

Yesterday
I sat at my piano
And wrote a song.
From whence did the melody come?
From what experience
Did I draw the words?

Who do I thank
For such a gift as this?
Is God the master
The originator
Of all creative thought?

Or is He my divining rod
That leads me
To the cool waters of thought
That subterranean well of inspiration
Where all creativity is born?

The veil is sometimes lifted
And I see the wizard's face
And know he is surely the source
But then, the apparition fades
And I am alone again.
Still, I cannot deny the touch
The warmth, the inner spark
When visited by that glow within
That divine gift, rare, and priceless
Of the creative fire.

Discovery
For Steven

Today
I walked the streets of London with you
Though hot the day
And tired and sore my feet
To Fleming's lab
Where first he toiled
With white coat
And petri.

All scientists
Kindred spirits
Searched the microscopic world
Of bacterium
For clues.

We found Alexander's lab
Dusty and ancient
Small and cramped
Yet preserved for humanity to see

That all may share
In the miracle discovered there
Penicillin!

You looked respectfully and lovingly
At his meager supplies
As though sacred
For, though old and outdated
The objects spoke
The magic of the tale:
The luck, the happenstance
The discovery of a millennia.

Now you
Also a scientist
Have taken up the challenge
Have pledged your oath
That, like Fleming, in 1928
You would "not neglect
An extraordinary appearance
Or happening."

So, critics and all
You have stood by your claim!
Your findings have revealed
Another miracle
One that will benefit
All mankind:
A simple antimicrobial
Silver nitrate
That, combined with fluoride varnish

Will eliminate tooth decay
On Planet Earth!
How utterly simple!
How utterly safe and painless!
How utterly remarkable!

We have walked in the footprints
Of a scientific giant today.
Yes, measured, and grateful, we have trod.
Passing over the threshold at Winsland Street
You turn to take in again
The wonder of this place!

Perhaps in years hence
Others will take pilgrimage
To a new scientific mecca
Where once you labored and toiled.

It is then
This visit to Fleming's lab today
Will be most meaningful:
For then you will unequivocally know
As Fleming did
That your search for truth
Was not in vain
But had great merit!
That through your insight and knowledge
Others would benefit!

Therein lies the invocation
Of the explorer of truth.
Therein lies the power of your discovery.

Stars

This morning early
I saw a constellation of stars
Crisp and white
Against the dark sky.

The Big Dipper
With its distinctive shape
Called to me
In an ancient dialect
As old as the universe.

It was a brief glance upwards
But so bright
Was the glow emitted
That I can close my eyes
Even now
And their images remain
Transfixed in my mind
Still.

Oh, morning sky
Wise men have followed
Your light!
Captains have charted
Their course
By your celestial map!

I look to you now
Overhead
And divine wisdom and direction
From your brilliance.
Guide me now
Until daylight's sun
Crests over the land
And leads me home.

God, Have You Forgotten Me?

I sit swaddled in blankets
In the comfort of my home
And ruminate about my life:
Nearly five years, now
Since the beginning of Steve's illness
With cataclysmic change
Yet again.

Who am I to question
"Why me?"
Who am I to judge the gravity
Of my personal travail
Rank it in the hall of human experience?

Am I living in the Gaza Strip?
Or a makeshift refugee camp in the Sudan?
Or the rubble of earthquake-ridden Haiti?
Who am I to complain?

God is Father to us all.
I remind myself.
He is watching over us all

Even the tiny sparrow.
There is much to be thankful for:

Tonight, I lay in my four-poster bed
Engrossed in Elie Wiesel's 'Night.'
I have not endured nor born witness to the horrors of
A Dachau or an Auschwitz!
There is food in my pantry and cupboards!
More clothes in my closet
Than I could wear out in a lifetime!
Let's put things in perspective here!
No "poor me!"

I breathe deep
Look at my husband reading beside me
And my little dog sprawled across the covers
And know, in truth
God has not forgotten me.
No, He has blessed me:

Steve has twice outwitted death
Our lives together have weathered and survived
The hurricanes, ravages, and lessons of life
Photographs abound bearing witness
To the continuous thread of family
We are connected to.

Forgotten? No!
Everywhere I turn is evidence that He indeed
Is mindful of me!

Going Deep

How deep can one go
Without disappearing
Without being swallowed
In the black
Without sinking into the realm
Of the lost?

I have traveled
To the mouth of the Styx
Without crossing over
Merely walked into its waters
Calm yet treacherous
Where the dead journey.

I have descended
Below the living
With deep thoughts of sorrow
Remembrances of grief
Days and nights
When hurricanes swept my shores
And ravaged my happiness.

How do I rise
Pull myself upward
From the depth that has swallowed me
Like a rogue wave a tiny boat?

Hear my cry, oh God
From the place within
This womb of darkness!
Hear my cry
Though it is faint and weak!
Hear its anguish
For the waves' thunderous roar
Tries to silence my voice!

Restore to life my spirit
Once rich with life and vitality!
Drag from the deep
This sodden soul
Who begs for respite
For she lives
And is yet
Too young to die!

One More Time

Let me see an apricot sunrise
And float down the mighty Colorado
One more time.

Let me wake to the music of the meadow lark
And walk the path through Lullwater
One more time.

Let me watch my grandchild's first step
And listen as coos turn into words
One more time.

Let me roll over and whisper, "I love you,"
As night sounds fill the air
And wake in the arms of my lover
One more time.

Let me walk the Magnificent Mile
And hear the sounds on Fifth Avenue
One more time.

Let me read Tennyson's 'Ulysses'
And hear Beethoven's 'Ninth Symphony'
One more time.

Let me see the sandy beaches
And steep cliffs of Bora Bora
And walk DaVinci's Florence
One more time.

Let me enjoy a beignet in New Orleans
And hear a southern drawl
One more time.

Let me read my children's
Letters of appreciation
And comfort my grown child who sorrows
One more time.

But most of all
Let me love life's unexpected pleasures
And find joy in every new day
One more time.

Words

Words
Like a net
Cast upon the water
Stretch far beyond you
Then return
From the heart of another.

Powerful and strong
They can edify
Or crucify
Amuse
Or afflict.

The essence
Of humankind's language
Words communicate
Our innermost thoughts
And our most basic needs.

How we use them
What we choose to say
Can sometimes become

A matter of life or death
Determine whether one survives
Or not.

Choose well
Your words
They speak for you
Utter your name
With every syllable!

The waters
Lay before you:
How will you cast
Your net?

Friendship

Can there be any blessing greater
Than having a friend?
A bent ear for sharing secrets?
A stooped shoulder bearing our pain?

There is magic and serendipity
In finding a friend
A chance encounter
A spoken word, however brief.

How could we bear life's injustices
Endure heartaches, fall in love
Bear children, bury a loved one
If there were no friend to witness life with us?

Show me a life that is friendless
And there is surely inestimable sorrow
Loneliness, bitterness, and pain
For life was not meant to be lived in a void.

Good friends are hard to find:
As rare as the Hope Diamond
As long suffering as Job
As timeless as a Chanel design.

I am grateful for my friends
Rich with grace
Long on mirth and laughter
Thank you for a lifetime of love
Thank you for being my friend.

Patriotic

The Patriot

Pick some flowers for me
For I have perished
And am no more.
Lay them on my grave
For all to see
That they may know
I left as a boy
But died as a man.

I fought valiantly
For a country
Whose ideals I believed in
And whose land I loved.
Cry no more for me
For, though I am gone
Your unborn children
Will unequivocally know
I died to save their right
To enjoy a life of freedom.

Hear me now
From deep within this tomb!
Know that I knew love
The love of familial bonds
And joy
Joy from a childhood free of fear
Where opportunities were abundant
To grow, to seek, to choose, to thrive!

I died to preserve these rights
For all Americans!
ALL AMERICANS!
White, Black, Latino
Muslim, Jewish, Christian!
That all who earn the right
To become Americans
Might share in her riches
And feast on her bounty.

Love her as I have loved her!
Cherish her!
Defend her!

For I have sacrificed myself
Upon her altar!
Her future now depends on you!

*Dedicated to my dad, the ultimate patriot, who loved his country
and defended her in time of war. He taught all five of his children
to love and cherish her, and value the freedoms we, as Americans,
enjoy.*

Thank you, Dad. I value you, as you taught me to value her.

Raise the White Flag

This cannot continue!
We cannot sustain another tragedy
More hateful rhetoric
The innocence of our children
Destroyed by fear!

We are complacent and apathetic
When we choose inaction:
The doors of Congress are barely open
The chairs of our justices remain vacant.
Where is the succor
For we Americans are weary!

This country is not theirs alone!
We, the people, throughout history
Has included WE, THE PEOPLE!
Diversity, like DNA, runs through
Every single American's veins.
Therein lies the truth:
That we are more alike
Than different!

Then, raise the white flag of peace
Peace among all people!
Cast off all impediments
For even a blind man can envision
And a deaf man dream!

We must adopt, once again
The qualities of character
That have made our leaders
And nation exceptional:
Love, restraint, inclusion
Compassion, wisdom
Insightfulness, and humility
For every single one of us
Is worth it.

Love

Our New Normal
For Steven

Does all change have its melancholy?
Must all change be a death
Of all that we have known?

It's said a person changes body cells
Every seven years.
And, yet, that body lives on
Unaware of the mighty reconstruction
Being wrought.
Can we not do the same?

Perhaps, someday
We will see the value of all our suffering
That was the change…
Perhaps this was just
A providential transformation
With the power to redirect and heal!

Perhaps, in the course of a lifetime
With change the only constant
We might adjust to the now
And find comfort in it.

To accept and be satisfied
Will not be easy
For we must vanquish the foe
That is reason…
For we are shortsighted
And cannot, with mortal eyes
Explain the why.

This is our new normal
A pledge at the altar:
In sickness and in health…

In all our longings
We must remember love
For purpose and devotion
Need not die.

The Way Things Stay
For Steven

Your broken flesh
Now healing
Ripples beneath my own
Dark and raised
And proud of the way our love
Has stayed grounded
Though torn and ravaged
By the winds of experience.

I have learned
That the how
Has replaced the why
Of loving you.

And though your body
Has been altered now
With scars littering your soft places
Yet my love

Remains constant
And unchanged:
A testament
To the way things stay.

You Are My Spring

Today, I saw a shooting star!
I walked barefoot in my garden
And wore a sleeveless dress and light sweater
For the first time in months!

All around me
Bedraggled-looking plants
Are sending shoots of green
Through thick layers of mulch
For the earth's season of slumber
Is coming to an end.

I have been in a perpetual state of winter
Since my love's passing
Frozen, alone, in a blizzard of grief
I am beginning the long thaw
When old, however familiar, must be forsaken
And new, embraced.

I am glad for this transition
Glad for you, with whose courage and compassion
I am now willing to replant hope

In my faithless heart
Replace love for one gone
With the promise of love for another.

You are my Spring!
I found you low to the ground
Planting daffodils and tulip bulbs
Hands deep within the soil.

You were not afraid of my fears!
You validated and acknowledged them
Though wearily at times
For you sought to know my truth
And see all of me.

For, when tears fell like rain
From the reservoir of my heart
Yet you held me tenderly to assuage my pain
Until the floodgates closed
And the rain receded.

Blessed Spring renews
With its green upon the land!
It is a gift of the earth
A joyful season
For you, my love, are in it!

Touch Me Now

Touch me now!
Do not let these angry words
Leach into your heart!
Do not let your thoughts
Rankle longer in ambivalence!
You must act now
Now, on our behalf!

Touch me now
Before your fingers
Lose their memory
And cannot find their way to me
Before all hope for recompense
Can be satisfied.

My days
Are agonizingly long now
Since first you left.
But the nights…
The nights are now unbearable
As I scan the sheets
For your sleeping form

Only to realize
You are gone!

How did this separation
Of spirit and soul happen?
How does a happy union
Fade and dissipate?
How does bright love
Dull and tarnish?

Touch me now
I beseech you
For my body longs for yours
Yearns to feel your familiar imprint
On my flesh
And smell your scent
Warm upon my lips!

Touch me now!

Lovemaking

Early morning
And sleepy still
I reach for you.
You respond
With a deep kiss
And arms spread wide
Welcoming me
With your embrace.

How many mornings
Have we lain
Side by side
And joined union.
Thirty-six years of yearning
Satisfied?

Through accidents
And illnesses
Children
And other distractions
I've still longed
For you.

In the stillness
Of my heart
And in the shadow
Of our often times
Harried lives
We have uttered love
On the wings of our desire
And found completion:

Lovemaking
Realized.

The Dance of the Naked

In my deepest night
You are the candle's brilliance
Enveloping me with light.
Embracing
Your feather wings surround
My spacious womb and
Breathe life into its vacancy.

Caress my soul
With your ancient wisdom!
Bless my heart
With the pure love of the ages
Songs sung in tune
Cadences cascading through
Tunnels of light and breath.

Oh be forever, my muse
Speaking truth in the hollows
Of your whisper:
The dance of the naked.

What If?

What if
The smiles of our grandchildren
Disappeared
Like morning dew
On summer grass?

What if
Our home
Our beloved abode
Was blown to the edge
Of all we had known
To the twilight of the universe
Never to be seen again?

What if your love for me
Lay silent on your lips
For a second too long
And the hurricane
That is my life

Engulfed me
And carried me away forever?
Too late…
Too late!

What if the thread
That binds us together
Like rising water
In a dam
Were to break
Under the deluged strain
Of silence and pain?
What if I no longer loved you?
What if this arterial bleed
Could not be stopped in time
And all we ever knew or loved
The sorrow and the joy
Bled out in anguished goodbye?

What if my life
No longer cast a shadow
On yours?
Would you notice?
Would you care?

I Am Your Home

In your vulnerability
I see a strength
Unmasked by change
And fate.

Because time will not
Remove all pain
Your indignant spirit
Cries out for justice
No man can give.

Know now, my love
I will stay with you
Though tentative
Your life's path.

I will not tread
On your dreams
For they are the ladder
That will guide us out of
The abyss.

Bury no hope.
Relinquish no pride
For you are my pride.

I will move beyond myself
And envelope you
With all my longings.
You will know the security
Of my heart and arms:
For I am your home.

You Are My Ocean

Wave caresses beach
Like a confident lover
Moving in closer
Resolutely
Swaying to the hallowed
Rhythm and cadence
Of a water drum.

Hear the tumble of the waves
Against the sand.
See the water's lacy film
Converge
And cover me.

For
You are my ocean
And I
Your land.
Together we join in tandem
Our longing

Churning water and sand
In the dance
Of yearning and fulfillment.

Hear our passion!
See our union:
Ocean's mighty power
And land's surrender!
For therein
Lies ultimate consummation!

The Long Goodbye
For Joni

The long goodbye has come…
Wrapped in a lifetime of memories
We sit by fireplace glow
And contemplate our blessed life together.

You and I have been an us, a we!
From the very beginning of our existence
You have been a part of me
Your effervescence and verve
Lighting with fire
My very passion for living!

How is it we have come to THIS, to NOW
When our indignant spirits
Are at war with an invisible foe
One that threatens our very world
As we know it?

There are no weapons of war
To annihilate this foe
And we are only a kingdom of two!
Our strength lies in our indefatigable love!

So, with that love
We will defend our fortress
For it has been a good home
A worthy abode!
Side by side
From the bastion of our hearts
We know what we must do…

Courage is often the offspring of heartache.
So, in deference to our pain
We will remain steadfast
For the duration of the battle
Look to each other in thanksgiving
For joy unmeasured
Abiding love unequaled!

Now, though fire's brilliance wanes
Its embers, with their steady glow
Warm us still, though war rages beyond.
Together we recollect all we have known
And settle in for the long goodbye.

Joy

This morning when I wake
There is a remnant of fading darkness
That collides with rays of glorious light
As they fall tenderly around your face.

I gaze at you
Still sleeping
And know we have chosen well
You, me, and I, you.

As today is our wedding day
Know now, my love
I will forever hold this radiant image of you
In my heart.
Your dreams and my dreams
Will join in a dance
Of happy union.

The past is but an island
To which we need no longer travel.
Only our future together lay before us
Perfect and serene.

My spirit and your spirit
Separate, yet entwined
Will forever share the secrets
Of our imaginings
No one else need ever know.

And now
As we marry
Pure joy distills upon this blessed moment
So rich with love and happiness.
Yes, today
Before God, angels, and witnesses
We choose each other.

For
I am yours
And you, mine.

The Choice

Tonight
When lights dim
And we savor stars
Like fine wine
We embrace our past
And consecrate our memories
In anticipation
Of tomorrow!

We will not cry over things
That never were
But rather hold hands
And in spoken unity
Pledge our faith in all
That can be.

In beauty
Rare and divine
Our eyes and hearts
Will lock in sacred trust
One for another
Our path's trajectory

Ever forward and onward
Will continue
Though at times rocky the shoal.

Tonight
There is no occasion for fear
For tested and tried
Has been our love
And the vanity and impatience of youth
No longer cloud our vision.

So, love
Lay by my side.
Let the ocean of love
And the scent of dreams
Wash over us!
Supplant the sorrow of imperfections
With the promises
Of perfect love eternal
For I choose you
As you have chosen me.

Self-Discovery

I Am Enough!
For Maya

In my sixty-first year
And still unknown
Even to myself
My voice
Loud and strident
Speaks out for others
But where is my savior?
Where is my own voice
That speaks for me, saying
"I am enough?"

Tears have fallen too long
Unchecked and without solace
From the one person
Who matters most.
They have formed rivulets of pain
Down my cheeks.
Canyons of self-condemnation.
I long to hear the words
The verbiage
Course down

No, seep down deep into my soul:
That my life lived on this earth
Has been of value!
No more sorrow, no more complaints
No more excuses!
Resolve: I will do the work
I was sent here to do!
Yet if my eyes are blind
How can I know I am worthy?
How can I see I am enough?

Will you walk the path with me?
Take the bandages from my eyes?
Reveal my real self—my worthy self?
In all my imperfections
My life matters!
I am worthy!
I am enough!
Help me God
To acknowledge the truth
And believe!

Quasar: My Star

I bent to another's will
Once again
Manipulation
And control
Their intent
Self-doubt and capitulation
The distressing outcome.

Surely
There will be no recompense
No apology.
My quasar, then
Will merely shine
Less bright.

So, there will be sorrow
In my universe
For a time
While I pick up the pieces
Of my brilliant star.

Where is my confidence
Of yesteryears
When first my star shone
In the firmament?
Who thought then
To light on fire
My wings?

I must obliterate
This force
That seeks to diminish
My happiness!
Oh then, heart
Cry no more!
Rehang then my star
In the heavens
For all to see
For neither fog nor cloud
Can obscure
Its luminosity
Nor eclipse its majesty!

So, I will shine on then
And let no other
Great or small
Shackle my will
Subdue my spirit
Or diminish my light.

Ah! Look there!
There shines my star
Visible, once again in the sky
Its zenith
Everlasting!
Its brightness and beauty
Celestial!
Look there!
It shines for me!

What Is My Destiny?

What is my destiny?
For when the foul winds of fate
Attempt to blow me off course
I must bear the strain
Set my sails for the struggle
And bring my vessel safely home.

Without a compass
Without a charted course
I am lost in an angry sea
Of indecision, doubt, and frustration.
Therefore, I must be steadfast
In my search for that course, tools in hand
That leads me to the center of myself
Where all is well, and good, and true.

Guide me then, oh God!
Make me a vessel of light
Upon these treacherous waters
That I may clearly see, without impediment

That true and everlasting path
For the seas are dark and deep
And I am frightened.

Bless me with a pure heart
And a discerning spirit
That I may follow, with faith in myself
My prescribed course
That I may come off conqueror in the end
That I may know unequivocally
Not just my vessel's superior workmanship
But its power and might and strength!

I see the shore of truth in the distance!
The waves are calling me from afar!
Before me lies my eternal home!
Bless this my ship, that
It may continue to carry me well
As I follow my true course
That it may in glory and victory
Guide me home!

Lifeline

I cry out from darkest chasm.
You throw me a lifeline
Down, down it falls
Into the pit
Where I crouch huddled
Against the cruelties and injustices
Of the breathing earth.

With experienced mind
And tempered emotion
You hoist me closer
To the teeming world of the living
My near-lifeless form
Cresting the edge of the pit
Eyes closed tight
Against the encroaching light
Of reality.

You comfort me with
Gentle words of encouragement
Lift my blinded eyes
Above the newborn light

And tell me the sunrise
Will not always be this frightful
This bright.

It is hard to trust your gift
So freely given
Hard not to hide in dark corners
In the safety of silence.
How can I know your lifeline proffered
Will lead to sustenance and life?
How do I know you are safe
To share secrets with?

You have thrown me a lifeline
Today, you are the only one
Who has responded to my guttural cries.
In faith, I hold tight to the rope
And with anxious heart
And trembling hands
Pull.

My Grown-Up Life

A short flight and I am back home
Back to my grown-up life.
It is a time of life I've thought of
Longed for, occasionally
As a bedraggled parent of four
Years ago.

How has my life unfolded?
What has it become?
Am I happy where I am
Proud of my path
Content to live it as it is now?

I planned for this!
This is the life I intended!
This my life
My sixty-year-old life!
Where has the time gone
For time has disappeared
Like fading sunsets
and youthful dreams?
What was I expecting?

I sit at my dining room table
And ponder, in totality
The extent of my living.
What have I learned?
What have I given?

I ask, really
One simple question:
What do I want my legacy to be?
What do I want to be remembered for
By those who know me?

My grown-up life, then
When personal dreams
Can finally be realized
And familial pull has lessened
Must count for something
Must be lived with purpose
And profundity!

Therefore, I pledge
To value each moment
Waste not opportunities for growth
Serve, be joyful, and live fully!

So, I will live with meaning
Use my heart and mind
To bless others
And heal wounds
Of broken dreams
From a childhood heart!

For, as the mortal pendulum
Swings beyond its median
And the quality of my living
Is taken into account
I will not waiver from my dreams
My chosen path!
I will succeed!
For I choose to continue living
An extraordinary life!

Like a Band-Aid

Yesterday
I came home
From another day
Of hard luck
And bad news.

With open arms and kind eyes
You enveloped me
Intuiting from the weary silence
My ragged condition.

My injuries
Appearing neither bloody nor bruised
Still begged for notice and attention.
Gently you assessed my wounds
Then placed your love upon them
Like a Band-Aid.

How could another
Perceive so clearly my want

And feel so keenly my need?
Had they themselves
Been hurt before?

Rarely
In the course of one's life
Is solace sought
And found!
Rarely
Is one's entreaty
Though silent
Heard!

Though the sufferers are many
And the saviors few
The gift of compassion proffered
Seeks not to destroy
But to restore
To tend to
Not to ignore!

So
In healing's perfect light
You have offered your love
Like a Band-Aid
And held and blessed my want
Like a perfect prayer.

I Have Given All My Energy Away

I am empty
Wiped out
Exhausted
Without spirit, for
I have given all my energy away.

I have thought of others first
Their comforts considered above my own
Their needs met
Their every wish granted.
Consequently
I have given all my energy away.

Is it not unwise
To empty my own cup
Bone dry?
Deplete my own well
When there is a drought in the land
And no rain in the forecast?

Can I not take for myself
What is needed
What is required
And proffer to others the surplus
Like a wise steward saves for winter
From summer's bounty in root cellars?

I must discern
And quickly
What path my weary soul must take
For gone are all surpluses!
Gone are the root cellars of my soul, for
I have given all my energy away.

I must nurture my heavy heart
My weary soul
Give succor and solace to my body
For all parts have suffered the sacrifice.

I must rise up and not fall down!
I must count myself among
The receivers of the gift of compassion
For I am worth it!

Depression

Depression is not who I am.
It is what I feel.
It takes my thoughts
And crumples them
As if a piece of aluminum foil
That, though straightened
Can never really be smooth again.

The fragility I feel now
Makes me bone weary
Osteoporotic tired
Without energy
Joyless
Robbed of sun
Rained on, cloudy
Flatlined
Without form, shapeless.

I see only tones of gray
For my technicolor world
Has been bled of life.
The colors still surround me

But they are as invisible to my eye
As day is to night.

Focus? What focus?
Easy for the normal person
To set goals, focus on the now
Plan for the future.
Putting foot before foot
Is such an effort
Easier to stay beneath covers
And seek succor within the cocoon.

Doing, being is such a chore.
An everlasting chore!
It is a wound so large
There is no bandage
Large enough to cover it.

I go to sleep hoping
That when I wake
The ache will be gone
The pain I feel
Will have vanished
Like following a deluge
That a rainbow in its stead
Might cover my heart.

But instead
I wake in the morning
The afternoon
Whenever

And the leaden burden
Still weighs on my chest
Like an elephant
And I cannot breathe!

I am assured by my doctor
This depression I now feel
Will soon pass.
So, with heavy heart
And labored breath
I sigh, and wait.

Nature

Tulips

Yesterday
I stood in a field of tulips
Acres of color
Unrestrained and free.
How is it that this riot of color
This full-spectrum palette of flowers
Cheers and pleases me so?
Why does my heart, open and yielding
Sing so joyously and strident
When surrounded by the tulips' brilliance?

I walked the muddy paths
In boots rarely worn
Waiting for the moment I'd don them
The tulip fields calling me
From hundreds of miles away
To come! To see!

Swallowed up and surrounded on all sides
By their colored opulence
And, so stately in their coats of many colors
I walked among the tulips

Their rows neatly ordered
By broad swaths of chroma!

I felt oddly at home among them
Though throngs of people
Meandered the cracked, spongy roads
And lines of color were diminished and broken
By the chaotic cavorting of children
Whose steps were punctuated
By the scurrying of exhausted parents.

Photographers
Earnest and attentive
Set up their shots
While field hands warned visitors
To stay on the paths
And not pick or harm the flowers.
I watched my daughter and grandson
Take in the beauty
Breathe it in as though an exotic perfume
Then snap a photograph of the scene
And move on.

I will remember our trip to RoozenGaarde
Many years, hence
When I am anxious for grandchildren and Spring
When the drabness of Winter
Explodes beyond the horizon
And the tulips, on the wings of Spring
Arrive once more!

The Dawning

Calm
Peaceful
The dawning is just moments away.
Outside
The half-moon shines
Within an obsidian black sky
And the universe is yet awash
With a galaxy of stars.

What keeps the firmament
Affixed in the sky
Keeps it from crashing
Into Mother Earth's loamy bosom?
What keeps the quasars
From falling from their heavenly perch
And drowning in the oceans below?

Ah! Look there! To the east!
A small sliver of light
Has cut through the sinewy canyons

And cast a shaft of luminescence
Over newly visible hills and valleys
On earth below.

The moon's silhouette is now fading
Into cerulean blue
And the dawning
Rich and vibrant with color
Now awakens.

The Juniper

The juniper
Gnarled and steadfast
Stands majestically in the snow
Its broad, bending limbs
Outstretched in homage
To the heavens above.

As this wintry morning awakes
Wide shafts of light
Cut through its branches
Making jagged patterns
On the snowy ground below.

Hungry jack rabbits gingerly hop
On ice-packed snow searching for food
While deer feed on winter grasses.
Together they discover another of winter's offering
The low-lying juniper berries nearby
Ripe with winter's chill.
The juniper offers her fruit willingly
A sacrifice for the hungry foragers of the wild.

I love this tree
Ancient, unfaltering
With its rich scent
And singular beauty!
Where the landscape opens
Within the high chaparral of Central Oregon
There the juniper awaits
Dressed in its Coat of Many Colors
It beckons me home.

Settling In

Nighttime comes.
The sun sets over the horizon
And all within me
Body and soul
Tells me it is time
To settle in for the night.

Outside the twilight blue
Relinquishes her hue
To the blackness of night
And all creatures great or small
Retreat to their womb-like nests
To slumber.

How does the earth know
Where to place the firmament
Or what color to paint her
Or where?
Will the stars be hung tonight
In the North or South, the East or the West?
Will clouds obscure their brilliance?

I look up into the night sky
And though its total darkness
Sweeps the ground
Its stars are high overhead
And are truly light years away.
Will time travel
Someday unite us
Earth and sky?

Settling in
At this day's end
There is time for repose
To rest from our labors
Time for reflection
To give an accounting of the day
And assess our place in the universe.
In the grand scheme of living
It is a time to dream!

Death

Feel the Warmth

Feel the warmth
Before it is gone!
Touch the skin
The heart
The love
One last time
Before it ebbs away.

The body's warmth
Is but an earthly reflection
Of a temporal state
For the inner spirit
That hidden passageway
Lives on
Beyond mortal flesh.

Does this comfort
Those who grieve
Ease as sorrow
Becomes loss?

Feel the warmth
For though the chill of death
Lingers ever near
Fingers have memory, too
Long after Autumn's dawn
Becomes Winter's night!

Seasons

Summer
The season of plenty
When sun and earth are one
Is ending, and will soon disappear
Bringing Fall
With its colorful leaves
Cooler temperatures
And icy ground.

Last week
When the sun hid while Fall's rain
Pressed against the clouds
And washed away the layers of dust
From the walk
You quietly left us.

It was in this late summer season
When burning sidewalks
Yielded to rain
Leaving detritus sodden on the ground
The sky opened up
And bore you Heavenward.

At dawn, today, we have gathered
Your family, all of us
With umbrellas opened
As well as hearts.
And, with the pouring of the rain
We, too, have shed volumes of tears
Human rain that has coursed down our cheeks
Forming rivulets of pain
That have now puddled at our feet.

We did not ask for this!
We cannot find justification, nor logic
In your swift departure
And it sits heavy on our hearts
And rankles our sensibilities!

Yet, as we sit beneath this canopy
Our thoughts travel over the miles
We have trod together
And joy mingles with sadness
As we ponder our familial love for you
And our now grievous
Inestimable loss.

We will never forget you!
And, as this day of remembrance
Draws to a close
With the cool breeze at our necks
We unitedly bow our heads in thanksgiving
For the blessing of having known you
That, though you left us

In the summer of your life
Our indefatigable bond
Will live on forever
Far into the remaining seasons
Of our earthly lives
And into light eternal.

Together

The day is barely dawning.
Careful not to wake you
I pull the sheets off
And lumber towards
The bedroom door.

I glance once more
At your sleeping form
And wonder how many mornings
We have left to share
How many nights we have left
To lay in each other's embrace.

You and I have been
An us, a we, a they.
Together
We have raised a family
Become grandparents.

We have laughed through
Most of life's lessons
And cried during the moments

Of greatest loss.
But always, we've done it
Together.

Now
We face the greatest challenge
Of our mortal lives
When you will
Reach beyond the veil
And let go of my hand.

Who will be with me then
For we have always traveled through
Happiness and sadness
Together.
Who will hold me, comfort me
When you are gone?

As winter's heavy rain
Beats down outside
Within
Clarity of thought
Distills upon my heart and mind:

All your words
Your irresistible smile
Your countenance
I've memorized.
They are emblazoned forever
On my wall of time.
You will be there for me like always

For as long as your image
Remains in my heart
You will be with me.

Know now I will be okay
Though the longing will be great
And the sadness and loss
Will be unutterable at times.

Please know I will always love you!
Thank you for blessing me
With your life, your love
Your loyalty, your mirth.

You are, and will forever be
The love of my life

Your Dee Dee.

Nothing Is Ever Lost

The day dawns gray and cold
The ice and snow have melted.
All around, the soggy earth reminds us
It is winter.

Last night we said goodbye
To our dear friend Ed.
For days he has wrestled with death
Fought it
As though a formidable foe.
Last night, that battle was lost.

But Whitman said:
"Nothing is ever lost
Or can be lost"
That an ember can flame again!

Do we believe?
Everyone wants to believe this
Who's suffered the death of a loved one
That, though the body turns cold as snow
It will surely live warm and vibrant again!

Do we leave this thought
To the theologians to grapple with?
What does our heart tell us?
What promises do we remember
What do we know from before our birth?

For most, there is no recollection.
No experience to cling to.
So, we watch our loved ones
Take their last breath
And wonder where the fire
That is their soul
Goes.

When the winter of their life comes
All we know for certain
Is that their body dies
And their essence—their spirit
Is set free.

Nothing is ever lost?
Much IS lost for those who love
For this life is all we know!
We must rely on memories and photographs
To remind us of those who've traveled
Beyond the veil.
That is somehow never enough.

Yet
We are there for our loved ones when death comes
Though it grieves our hearts

And, in faith, we hope they will be there
When we pass from this mortal realm.
It is then, they will welcome us home
When the great rekindling of love's ember
Will burn bright once again
And that which was lost, will be regained.

Evergreen

Morning's light remains hours away
And darkness, like a shroud
Still blankets the sky.
The chill in the air reminds me
It is indeed winter.

A dear friend who
Under pall of darkest night
In glory and beauty
Will leave her earthly home
Shoot across a star-filled sky like a comet
And pass through the veil of the living
Into light eternal.

What will she be remembered for
During her sojourn here
For, though erudite and brilliant
A profound and distinguishing feature of hers
Was humility
Believing others had more to teach her
Than she them.
A savior to many over the years

She has been wise and compassionate
And offered her vast knowledge and experience
To all.

For her children
Her soul's fading light
Will be a grievous loss!
To her husband, her passing
Will be wrought with unbearable sorrow and longing!
Yet her zenith
That point in the sky directly above him
Will yet be constant and bright
For her spirit's fire will never grow old
But will remain evergreen.

Faith

My wife, the love of my life is gone.
Her once-vibrant spirit
Brilliant mind
And agile body
Is no more.
The pall of death hangs heavy in the room
Where once she lay
The silence in our home now deafening.
I am bereft
For my heart has been rent asunder!

How can I go on living when she
My companion, my bride of nearly fifty years
Has passed beyond this mortal coil
And I am left to pick up the fractured pieces
Of a life of we, they, and us?

As this unwelcome reality sets in
Grief fills the recesses of my mind
And an angry voice, shrill and impudent
Screams for me to curse God and die
As Job once did!

On one hand
Her death is undeniable and unequivocal.
Yet try as I might
I cannot accept this truth
The finality of it
For it presses hard on my chest
And I cannot breathe!

On the other hand
I desperately cling to an abstraction
Lodged in my memory from a life before her:
FAITH!
All rational thought laid aside
I realize that FAITH, with all its mysteries
Is all that is left me
For I know no absolutes:
I am not privy to the workings of God
Nor the circumstances of the future.

I will do what I must to see her again
I must see her again!
I so want to believe this is possible!

What, then, must I do
To relinquish my long-held belief
That this earth life is all there is?
Must I look beyond the knowing
The tangible, the visual
To the realm of the unknown?

Perhaps immersing myself
In religious practice once again
Would be a comfort and perhaps a reawakening…
It was not so long ago that I, a priest
Drew into my heart and mind
The promises of God and eternity.
Could I not believe again
For my sorrow and longing
Consumes me with this desire.

Perpetual anger is menacing
And cursing God I must not do
For I need His help!
Fervently, on bended knee
I offer a prayer:
Introspective and sincere
I ask not just for solace and succor
But for FAITH
Pure and clear
Like water from a mountain spring.

His answer is swift and irrefutable:
I must bide my time
Sow the seeds of humility and wisdom
And nurture these offspring of FAITH
Through the growing season
After which, I will harvest the field's bounty.

So, I will patiently wait.
I will come to her when FAITH has been
Tempered and nourished

Through seasons of work and trial
When winter's field has been laid fallow
And following Spring's nurturing rains
And Summer's sun.
It is then we will reunite.
Eternity will stretch before us
Glorious and welcoming!
The reflection of our refulgent and matchless joy
Will shine in the brightest stars!
We will join hands once again
And walk into the light, together.

Shine On!

High overhead you now shine
In a galaxy of stars
Overlooking the earth
Where once you lived.

It has been nearly two years
Since your brilliance and vivacity
Faded from this life
Like an errant firework that flickered out too soon
Or a full moon obscured by heavy fog.

How I have missed you
My lover, my light!
How bright you once shined
In my earthly constellation of friends!
How rare was your effervescence!
How pure and uncluttered your visage!

Shine down upon me now
From your vantage within the firmament!

For, though your flesh is cold
Your spirit remains vivid and warm
And I know it still.

I carry on without you, dear
Yet all your smiles
And spoken words of yesterday
Are still crystalline and clear
Though age and memory dim.

Ah!
Looking off into the distance
I see your star rising now against the night sky
Brilliant beyond all the other stars above!
Your light, as in old days
Moves me onward.

I settle in for the duration of my days
And whisper to you in the vast Universe
The now-familiar words
"You are still my only star!
Shine on!"

Marcus' Poetry

Spilling the Ink of My Soul

Spilling out my soul
Like a drop of ink falling unformed and plain
Onto a blank piece of paper

Completely bare at our birth
We guide the stain
Following the same pattern for some
Creating an abstract new design for others
This is the story of our lives
And we draw it out with our own two hands
Making an unknown piece of art that cannot be appreciated
until it comes to fruition
Blindly we draw
Similar to many
Eventually producing complex uniqueness that only you
can truly see
Understanding is hidden
Yet your subconscious knows but will not tell

Lost in the drip-drop of the ink
Letting the world take control
Creating a different and foreign design

Losing sight of the grand scheme of our design
Most feel doubtful
Lost, overwhelmed, and far from hopeful
Yet some learn to reach out from the mundane stain that defines us
And take hold of the instrument that writes our lives
To tell the story that they want the world to hear
To become the change they wish to see in this world
To become the future and help those lost in the flood of chaos and uncertainty.

Fury, Terror, and Beauty

It cannot be foreseen
You will not know when it comes
Fury, terror, and beauty
Waiting for the storm to come
One moment you will bask in the sun
Gazing into the breaks of light
While in another you will watch the darkness overtake you
When that storm comes, fear not
Close your eyes
Reach out towards the sky
Listen to the raw power of the fury
Nothing is more powerful
Nothing is more elemental

We are but a mere speck of sand wandering from place to place
Destined to travel this world
Tormented by the all-enveloping power and darkness of the bellowing clouds
But as you close your eyes and reach on high
Feel the essence of the electricity building in the sky
Open your mind

Open your soul
And release yourself unto this world
Scream out into the storm
DO YOUR WORST!
FOR I WILL DO MINE!
And feel the shockwave explode from deep within you
Watch the world tremble
Shake the very foundation of everything you have come to
know
And wash your pain away with a tear.

On the Fear of Change

Tears roll down my face
Bleeding out my frustration, pain, and anger
All that was familiar
Is far from view
Everything I do is so different
Abstract, strange, and askew
This new world can be frightful
Yet I put my hand out and reach into the darkness
Like a lost child not knowing where to turn
I feel so afraid at times
Unknown and startling new thoughts fill the mind
Infecting and overpowering
Putting forth a feeling of lack of control
Yet as I reach out into the depths
I run forward as fast as I can
Breaking all barriers and obstacles in my path
Lost with no light to lead me
I learn to guide my own path
Becoming the darkness of confusion and frustration
Finding ways to gain comfort with comprehension, honor,
and understanding

The old times
Flooded with disbelief, uncertainty, and lack of self
confidence
Shying in the face of diversity and possibility
Waiting for my path to be laid at my feet
Yet as I stand here at the crossroads
Watching the sands of time shift
I feel these ancient emotions
And know what must be done
This effort will not have been in vain
For I will make of my life what was destined to be done
Fear is a natural resistance
But the fire within me will purge my consciousness of
weakness
And set forth the dawn of a new age.

Choice Defines

Choice is your God-given right
A means of defining your personality and methods of expression
Following the path of indecisiveness
Leads to compromised judgment and character
Following the path of consistent self-belief in choice
Leads to honor, development of personality, and integrity
By deviating from the troubles attributed to decision
We become self-conscious, weak, and untrue to ourselves
It is better to make the wrong decision and move forward
Than to remain stagnant with nothing to show in the way of accomplishment
Believe in yourself
Believe in the mystery of life
Follow the change at breakneck speed
And bob and weave with whatever life gives you

Predicting where the journey ends
Leads to a mirage of someone you are not
Make that choice
Make that decision
Move forward and progress in life

For no matter which way you go
It will always be unique and true
To the everlasting desires of what you wish to achieve.

Destruction

Crazy, anarchy, mayhem
Breaking through the doors of hell
Death, destruction, malice
Shining through what mankind held
The end was once said to be near
Now the future is far from view
Destroying beauty
Shattering innocence
Man's creativity has betrayed us all
Wield it, yield it, till the end
Show it, grow it
Manipulating every biological aspect nature can rend
Spewing puss, exhaling blood
Death in the worst kinds of ways
Scary, frightening, terrifying
The truth that soon lies ahead
Losing vision, losing thought
Every single kind of pain that this virus has wrought
Replicating itself, breaking you down
Every single day
Millions buried in the ground
Rotten, mangled, malicious in nature

Was it the virus or the man who became the monster?
Devious and thoughtless
Prevention not found
Caution disregarded
When the gavel of judgment came down
The shroud was lifted and all were to blame
For the future is and always has been in our own two hands
We shape it, we mold it
Just how we see fit
We make it or break it
But please don't let it end like this
I pray with every single breath
That my future son's first won't be his last.

Do Not Rely on Outside Belief

For you will fly, falter, then fail
To do things not for yourself
Unleashes weakness like the strongest winds and gale
Do not for others but for yourself
Look through eyes that are none but your own
Perceive it as it was meant to be seen

Asking others for the proper method of execution
While not believing in your own
Produces a flickering shadow of your own determination
Ask not what you should do or how it should be done
But determine for yourself which path is righteous and consistent with none
Follow the path of the unbeaten road
Produce a vision like none have ever seen
Open the eyes of comprehension and creativity of all those that surround
And show them what elaborate plan your mind can rend
Unique to all, understood by many
Your new views will show us the way

Do not rely on false visions
Nor should you let them pry
It is your mind that should be shown
This is your future
Your decision
Your life
So do everything in your power
To make it your own.

Drugs

Drugs can turn your greatest companion
Your greatest friend
Into an only partially existing image of their previous selves
It's a shame to watch them diminish
Into a phantom-like state
Becoming less and less expressive and true
Vicious cycles
Repeat consistently
Breaking all senses of hope and life
Controlling
Demanding
Feeding on your very soul
Cannot escape
This blackhole of self-hate
Break free of this curse
Reach out and grab my hand
To the essence of life that can bring more joy than any drug
mankind or nature can rend
I will show you the way
I will raise you above
Bring you to your inside voice
That will bring you back to salvation

I can only open the door
It is up to you to walk through
But do not feel afraid
Because it is your true life that awaits you.

Motto of Science

The motto of science
The models that are used
Innocent creatures that have no choice
Genome altered, physically deformed
All for the purpose of knowledge
To save a life, one must be lost
But the question is, at what cost?
Impossible to learn complex mechanisms
From microscopically small unicellular organisms
Dabbling from flat worm to mouse
Rabbit to dog
All viewed as less in the eyes of man
But whoever said that animals don't have a soul?

I feel the pain every time I look into their eyes
Knowing what's coming
Knowing where their fate lies
Death by an invisible gas
Gasping for air that has all but vanished
Lights slowly dim and suddenly they're silenced
I understand the pain and understand the cost
And know what benefits result

I accept what must be done to let disease affect none
But all I ask is respect and appreciation
For those lives that were abruptly and forcibly taken.

Music

Music
Inspiring
Driving
Provoking instantaneous state of mind
Unique yet felt by all
All encompassing
All understanding
Fulfilling yet at times can reveal the gaping hole present
Can bring forth pain
Can bring forth joy
The plethora of feelings and lack thereof
Present, absent, lingering

Flick the switch and a new world unfolds
The thought existing in the now fades out into nothingness
You become that moment, the beat, the phrase, the emotion
Feel it take you
Feel it break you
Simply feel it and let it show you a story like no simple
words on paper can tell.

Path of Self-Realization

Confusion
Finding oneself
Bathing in a ball of flame
Surrounded and consumed
Lost in the darkness yet blinded by the light
Walking with the shadows
To find some sense of comfort and altered reality
The flame always follows
Persistent and never ending
Representation of the haunting past that always lingers
It will never go away
Shutting your eyes will not make it disappear
Running away only feeds it with fear
Open your eyes, open your mind
And your soulful effort to face your fear will extinguish your burden
Become the flame, become the shadow, become the darkness
Face it with every attribute that defines you
And manifest your own path of enlightenment and determination
For none other than you can open that door

Do not rely, do not hide to cry

Be yourself and the puzzle of discovery will unravel.

Stop the Running

With the speed and agility
To outrun any foe
Phantom, memory, people alike
We use our strength
What little we have left
To leave behind that piece of ourselves
That cursed and poisoned our souls
Run, run, far, far away
Becoming someone new
Yet unbeknownst to yourself
The consistent strength still always resided within
Change the surroundings, change the people
The pain and issues will still remain
Change where you sleep, change who you meet
It will all be one but the same
Run, run, far, far away
Just to try and fight another day
Run, run, far, far away
No matter where you go, you cannot escape
Time will not change the pain
It will not bend anything to your gain
You must seize it, control it, feel it, use it, learn from it

For without wisdom, we are but beasts
Going wherever our emotions take us
Feel them make you, feel them break you
Consuming, overwhelming, comforting, empowering
Let not this false view persuade you
View the world in its entirety
See it for what it truly is
Do not run, do not hide
Breathe in your fears
Breathe in your hatred
Breathe in your pain
Learn, become, visualize, prophesize, REALIZE!
Stand in front of them all
Take no more and give nothing back
Stand for yourself, for all you are, for everything you believe in
Become one with yourself and do not stray
Even when your life is in constant disarray.

What Drives Us

What do we strive for?
What drives us?
What makes us push past that moment of truth?
That defining moment that expresses purity of soulful
expression
Why push forward?
Why push back?
Does it change who we are, or the way we are treated?
Is it our strength that is seen through all barriers of
prejudice, segregation, and fear?

It is this very moment, today, now
That we must seize and demand more from
Never is it enough to live sedentary
Never is it enough to not evolve
For if you do what you've always done
You'll always get what you've always gotten
Perhaps the consciousness you have come to know has
forgotten
While your subconscious knows but does not tell
Like the wise man Mahatma Gandhi once said:
"You must be the change you want to see in this world."

I HOPE YOU ENJOYED THESE POEMS!